ABOUT TIME

Calendars

Brian Williams

SMART APPLE MEDIA

First published by Cherrytree Press
(a member of the Evans Publishing Group)
327 High Street, Slough
Berkshire SL1 1TX, United Kingdom
Copyright © 2002 Evans Brothers Limited
This edition published under license from
Evans Brothers Limited.

Created and designed by
THE FOUNDRY DESIGN AND PRODUCTION
Crabtree Hall, Crabtree Lane, Fulham, London, SW6 6TY

Special thanks to Vicky Garrard and the late Helen Courtney

Published in the United States by
Smart Apple Media
1980 Lookout Drive
North Mankato, MN 56003

Printed in Hong Kong

Library of Congress Cataloging-in-Publication Data

Williams, Brian, 1943- Calendars / by Brian Williams.
p. cm. — (About time) Summary: Explores the history of the calendar
as it relates to time-keeping in general, touching on lunar and solar
years, almanacs and diaries, time zones and the International Date
Line, and famous dates.
ISBN 1-58340-207-1
1. Calendar—Juvenile literature. [1. Calendar.] I. Title.
CE13 .W45 2002   529'.3—dc21   2002023106

2 4 6 8 9 7 5 3 1

Acknowledgments

The author and publishers would like to thank the following for permission to reproduce
Photographs: Front cover and Title page R. Frerck/Robert Harding Picture Library and Foundry
Arts page 4 (bottom) Archives Charmet/Bridgeman Art Library page 5 R.Frerck/Robert Harding
Picture Library page 6 (top) Bob Firth/International Stock/Robert Harding Picture Library
(bottom) Topham Picturepoint page 7 Peter Arkell/Impact page 8 British Museum/Bridgeman
Art Library page 9 (top) Whitford & Hughes/Bridgeman Art Library (bottom) Topham
Picturepoint page 10 (top) Michael Freeman/Phototake NYC/Robert Harding Picture Library
(bottom) Bob Firth/International Stock/Robert Harding Picture Library page 11 (bottom) The Art
Archive/British Museum page 12 (top) Mary Evans Picture Library (bottom) Science
Museum/Science & Society Picture Library, page 13 Nigel Francis/Robert Harding Picture
Library page 14 (top) Bridgeman Art Library/Vatican Library, Rome (bottom) Dr Fred
Espensk/Science Photo Library page 15 The Bridgeman Art Library/National Gallery, London
page 16 (top) Bridgeman Giraudon/Lauros (bottom) John Ross/Robert Harding Picture library
page 17 Pinacoteca Capitolina, Palzzo Conservatori, Rome/Bridgeman Art Library page 18
Selborne Church, Hampshire/Bridgeman Art Library, page 19 (top) Robert Harding Picture
Library (bottom) Caroline Penn/Impact page 20 (top) Topham Picturepoint (bottom) Roger-
Viollet, Paris/Bridgeman Art Library page 21 Ken Walsh/Bridgeman Art Library page 22
Bridgeman Art Library page 23 (top) Bridgeman Giraudon/Lauros (bottom) Historical Society
of Pennsylvania/Bridgeman Art Library page 24 (top) Rob Francis/Robert Harding Picture
Library (bottom) Topham Picturepoint page 25 Giraudon/Bridgeman Art Library Page 26 (top)
S.Villager/Explorer/Robert Harding Picture Library (bottom) Private Collection/ Bridgeman Art
Library page 27 Topham Picturepoint page 28 (top) Valder Tormey/International Stock/Robert
Harding Picture Library. All graphics (4, 11, 28, 29) are courtesy of Foundry Arts.

Contents

Introduction

WHAT IS A CALENDAR?

Do you know the time? What's today's date? When is New Year? To answer the first question you need a clock or watch; to answer the other two, you need a calendar. Like a clock, a calendar measures how time passes. We think of a calendar as having numbers (the days in a month) and words (the days of the week, the names of the months). A diary is a kind of calendar. Both are so much a part of our lives that most people could not imagine life without them: how would we organize our lives?

Every new year, people start a new calendar or diary. Calendars help us to organize our work and leisure time, and remind us of special days, such as birthdays and holidays. The calendar the majority of us use today took 1,000 years to perfect.

PEOPLE KEEPING TIME

For thousands of years, people measured time by the daily rising and setting of the sun. Sun time gave them "today," "yesterday," and "tomorrow." The changing moon, passing from new to full and back again every 29.5 days, gave

them "months." The passing of the seasons (spring, summer, autumn, winter) gave them the "year." Knowing when summer was about to give way to autumn meant people could plan ahead and gather in stores of food for the winter. A calendar was therefore very useful.

People first found they needed calendars around 5,000 years ago. By this time

Medieval farmers worked to the seasons. This picture, from 1490, shows plowing and sowing: tasks for springtime.

many people had become farmers and had started to live in towns. Some people could read and write and they used this newly developed skill to keep records of crops and taxes and to write lists of kings, laws, battles, and gods. Calendars told people the right times to do all kinds of things (such as collecting taxes or carrying out a religious ceremony). Numbering the years gave people a sense of history: they knew, for example, when their country or city was founded.

KNOWING THE RIGHT DATE

Although time differs from country to country (daytime in the United States is nighttime in Australia), we all use a 24-hour clock. Today most people also use the same calendar with 365 days in a year, and wherever you go in the world, most calendars show the same year-date. In a world of jet travel and Internet commerce, it makes sense to use the same system.

The common calendar was established by Christians, who started counting years from the birth of Jesus Christ. In this system, we write A.D. 1900 to mean 1,900 years after that event which marks the start of the Christian or Common Era (an era is a very long period of time); 1900 B.C. means 1,900 years before the birth of Christ. Other calendars still in use include those of Muslims, Jews, and the Chinese, and many ancient peoples had their own calendars.

It seems simple enough. If people want to know the time, they look at a clock. If they want to know the date, they look at a calendar. The trouble was, making a calendar that worked properly took thousands of years, and it's still not quite right. This book takes a look at how some early calendars were made, and how we ended up with the calendars we use today. It explains why we have a New Year and other special days, and why calendars have sometimes caused not only puzzlement but riots in the streets!

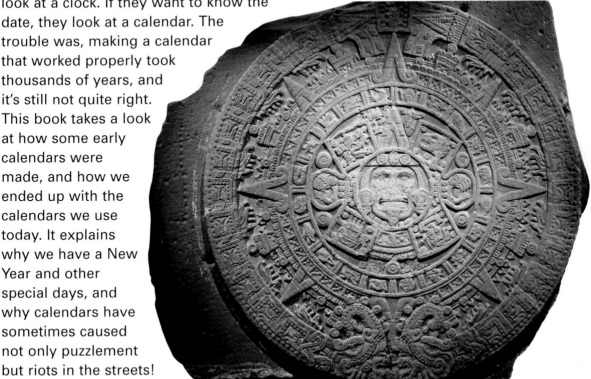

This massive Aztec calendar stone from Mexico is twice as wide as a person. The central pictures show four previous "world endings": the Aztecs believed the world was destroyed and reborn over and over again.

The Sun and Moon

THE FIRST CALENDARS?

Archeologists have found animal bones with markings scratched on them which date from around 30,000 years ago. Could these be the very first calendars? It is possible that Stone-Age people may have made these markings to count the days. But Stone-Age hunters, who wandered from place to place, did not really need a calendar: they lived their lives by the seasons.

 Before people had clocks, they used the sun as a timer. Sunrise meant go to work, sunset meant go to bed. The sun was the all-powerful giver of life.

WHO NEEDED A CALENDAR?

The first real calendars were made about 5,000 years ago. By then people were farming the land. Farmers needed to be sure of the right time to plant seeds; they needed to know when to expect the first rains; and they needed to be prepared for when the first autumn frosts might strike.

Religion had also become an important part of people's lives. Priests needed to know exactly when important ceremonies should take place.

So how did people start making a calendar? Many ancient peoples believed in gods represented by the moon and the sun. The moon and the sun were heavenly "clocks" that all could see, and they seemed to move to a regular rhythm. So moon time and sun time were used.

COUNTING IN MOONS

The moon comes back to the same position in the sky about every 28 days. The Ancient Sumerians and Babylonians,

The Ancient Egyptians worshipped the sun as the god Ra or Re, shown here with another god named Anubis. Every day Ra traveled across the sky in his sun boat.

MEASURING A DAY

When does your day begin? When you wake up? For the Ancient Greeks, the day began at sunset. For an Ancient Egyptian, day began at daybreak, or sunrise. The Romans decided to make midnight the end of one day and the start of the next, and we still use this system today.

In the ancient world, not everyone counted in days. The peoples of northern Europe counted in nights. British people still speak of a "fortnight," meaning "14 nights."

who lived in Mesopotamia (modern-day Iraq), were the first peoples to make a calendar based on these moon cycles, or "months."

Unfortunately, the moon is not a reliable clock. It is the Earth's movement around the sun that determines the time between one spring season and the next, the period we call a "year."

COUNTING BY THE SUN

The ancient Egyptians studied the sun with particular interest. Their chief god was the sun god Ra. They worked out a year with 12 months, each with 30 days (making a total of 360 days). Then they added five extra days, which, so the story goes, were given by the god Thoth. So the Egyptian year had 365 days, which was exactly right—almost.

Many ancient peoples worshipped the sun and kept watch on its passage across the sky. In Britain, the famous standing stones at Stonehenge were set up between 2950 and 1600 B.C., and this was probably the site of ceremonies linked to the rising and setting of the sun.

Stonehenge was a sacred place for observing the sun. Today people still gather here to watch the sunrise at midsummer.

A Year of Seasons

WHO NEEDS YEARS?

Most people in ancient times did not need to know which year it was. Ordinary people may not have marked yearly events such as birthdays. Instead, they marked time by "moons" or by the seasons (spring, summer, autumn, winter). A child might be "five summers" old; an old person might have lived "many winters." People counted in family generations, as we see in the Bible, which has long lists of fathers and sons.

The start of a ruler's reign was often used as the beginning of a calendar: "so many summers since King Bodnacherib was crowned." People also counted time from an important event, such as "so many moons since the plague of locusts" or "so many winters since the war with the Spartans." They relied on memory, on stories told by the old to the young.

Astronomer-priests worked out the length of a year by observing the sun. The Egyptians had another clue: the river Nile. This is the world's longest river and the world's oldest calendar.

A carved stone from Mesopotamia showing the conquests of King Sargon of Akkad, who ruled during the 2300s B.C., a time when a ruler's reign marked the beginning of a calendar.

RHYTHM OF THE RIVER

The Nile flooded every year. When its waters rose, people recorded the highwater mark on poles set in the riverbank. When the floodwaters fell, they counted the days until the water rose once more to reach the highest mark on the pole. This happened around 365 days later.

The Egyptians also found another year-sign, this time in the night sky: Sirius or the Dog Star. Once a year this very bright star was in line with the rising sun. The Egyptians watched to see when the star appeared at daybreak over the top of a

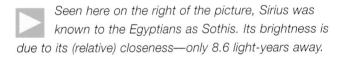
The Nile in flood, the yearly event on which farming in Egypt relied. Dams now prevent the Nile from flooding, the first of which, the High Dam, was built in 1902.

tall obelisk (a stone pillar) which faced east, toward the sun. Remarkably, this was the same day that the Nile rose to its highest point. The day when both these events occurred became the Egyptian New Year.

GETTING IT ALMOST RIGHT

The Egyptians soon realized that the sun year was not exactly 365 days—it was six hours, or one quarter of a day, longer. Adding on the extra time to make a leap year every four years, or as an extra-long day once a year, would have made the Egyptian calendar almost perfect. But the powerful priests of ancient Egypt would not agree to adding any "artificial" time to the calendar, so it was left to "drift" by six hours every year.

Seen here on the right of the picture, Sirius was known to the Egyptians as Sothis. Its brightness is due to its (relative) closeness—only 8.6 light-years away.

KEY DATES

▶ **4241 B.C.** First recorded Egyptian date
▶ **c. 2500 B.C.** Egyptians use three calendars; one for farming, one for government, and one for religious ceremonies
▶ **2400 B.C.** Sumerians use a year of 360 days (12 months of 30 days each)
▶ **587 B.C.** The Jews begin using the Sumerian-Babylonian calendar
▶ **432 B.C.** Meton of Athens works out a 19-year cycle to bring the lunar (moon) calendar used by priests into line with the solar (sun) calendar; it was accurate to five days over 19 years
▶ **150 B.C.** Hipparchus of Rhodes, a Greek scientist, calculates a year to be 365.242 days long; he also works out that a month is 29.53 days long

THE 11-DAY DIFFERENCE

The moon seems to be a perfect clock. It waxes and wanes (from new moon to full and back again) every month. Were moon time and sun time the same? To find out, astronomers in Egypt and Mesopotamia counted the days between one new moon and the next. A moon month lasted 29.5 days. So a moon year was 12 x 29.5 days. That was 354 days, not 365.

This 11-day difference gave calendar-makers a big problem. The sun year of 365 days gives the Earth its seasons, and people who stuck to a moon year calendar discovered that in a few years the calendar was way out of line with the seasons. A moon calendar was useless as a guide for sowing seeds or harvesting.

The moon shows us the same face all the time, but using it as a calendar posed all kinds of problems for people.

TRY A 19-YEAR CYCLE

To try to solve this problem, astronomers worked out a new system to link the moon and sun calendars. Their calculations indicated that seven years of 13 moon months followed by 12 years of 12 moon months were almost exactly equal (in days) to 19 sun years. This 19-year "cycle" was called the Metonic cycle, after a Greek astronomer named Meton, although the Babylonians and Chinese also used it. It brought the calendar back in time with the seasons.

The cycle still "ran fast" and to make the system work, the Greeks had to add 90 days to their calendar every eight years, while the Chinese added seven months every 19 years. Only clever mathematicians could make any sense of it at all!

HOW LONG IS A YEAR?

Most ancient astronomers believed that the sun circled the Earth. Today, we know that it is actually the other way around and that the Earth, like the other planets, circles the sun. The true year is the period of time it takes the Earth to orbit the sun once. This is the year on which our calendar is based, and it lasts 365 days, 5 hours, 48 minutes, and 46 seconds. That's 365.242 days. There is another year, used by astronomers, called the sidereal or star year. This is a little longer—365 days, 6 hours, 9 minutes, and 11 seconds.

Winter—Plow in the stubble

Spring—Sowing

Summer—Growth

Autumn—Harvest

The four seasons ▲

THE SEASONS

Matching sun time with the seasons is tricky, since the seasons are not the same all over the world. In the tropics, there are two seasons (wet and dry). In places farther north and south of the equator, there are four seasons—spring, summer, autumn, and winter. In ancient Egypt, there were three seasons: flood, seed sowing, and harvest time.

People looked to nature to tell them when the seasons were changing. Around 800 B.C., a Greek named Hesiod wrote about the signs people used to tell that spring had arrived. When farmers heard the calls of migrating cranes, they knew it was time to plow the fields. When they saw snails climb plants, they knew it was time to stop digging in vineyards.

▷ *A Roman coin showing the two-headed Roman god Janus, after whom January (the "beginning month") is named.*

THE NAMES OF THE MONTHS—1

▶ **January** The name January comes from the Roman god Janus, god of doorways and beginnings; he is represented with two heads, one looking backward and the other looking forward

▶ **February** This month is named after the Roman festival of Februa, a time of purification

▶ **March** March is named after the Roman god of war, Martius, or Mars, as he is known in English

(see also pages 15, 17, and 19)

Days, Weeks, and Months

KEEPING WATCH

Before people used hours, they split the day into "watches." Watches were not all the same length: a day watch in summer was longer than a day watch in winter. In winter, night watches were longest. The idea of days, weeks, and months developed slowly, and in different ways.

A medieval peasant takes a sighting of the North Star to find north and south.

STAR-DAYS AND SUN-DAYS

There are two ways to measure the length of a day. One way is to record how the stars seem to move in the night sky. The time it takes for the stars to move once around the sky and return to their original positions (as seen by a person anywhere on Earth) is a sidereal day. It lasts 23 hours, 56 minutes, and 4 seconds. The word *sidereal* comes from the Latin word for "star."

The other way is to measure how the sun appears to move across the sky. From midnight to midnight is one solar day. A mean (average) solar day lasts 24 hours.

This clock, made in England in 1736, shows mean time (left face) and sidereal time (on the other 24-hour face). Clockmaking made great advances between 1500 and 1750.

SUMERIAN MATH WIZARDS

The Sumerians and Babylonians of more than 4,000 years ago were very advanced in their learning. Especially good at math, they worked out a calendar year of 360 days, with 12 moon months of 30 days each. Most ancient peoples counted in 10s, as we still do, but the Sumerians and Babylonians counted in 60s. Very little is known about these ancient cultures, so no one is sure why the number 60 was chosen, but it may explain why we have 60 minutes in an hour and 60 seconds in a minute.

WHY 24 HOURS?

Why are there 24 hours in a day? The use of the "magic" number 24 dates from the time of the Sumerians and Babylonians of Mesopotamia. By 2400 B.C., they had divided day and night into 12 hours each.

To measure hours, you need clocks. By 100 B.C. the Romans were using sun clocks and water clocks. They used hours as a measurement of time, but their hours were not all the same length—summer hours were longer than winter hours. It was not until much later, after A.D. 1000, that people began to use regular hours in everyday life and language.

The Tower of the Winds in Athens, Greece, was built in about A.D. 100 to keep time. It had a sundial on the sides and a water clock for days when the sun was not shining.

NAMING THE DAYS

People gave the days names. The table shows how our days of the week got their names. Most were taken from the names of gods or goddesses. In English, the days are a mixture of Roman names, such as Saturday (from Saturn's day), and Norse or Saxon names (Wednesday comes from Woden's day). *Dies* was the Latin word for "day."

Roman (Latin)	French	Saxon	English
Dies Solia	Dimanche	Sun's day	Sunday
Dies Lunae	Lundi	Moon's day	Monday
Dies Martis	Mardi	Tiw's day	Tuesday
Dies Mercurii	Mercredi	Woden's day	Wednesday
Dies Jovis	Jeudi	Thor's day	Thursday
Dies Veneris	Vendredi	Frigg's day	Friday
Dies Saturni	Samedi	Seterne's day	Saturday

Michelangelo's painting on the ceiling of the Sistine Chapel in Rome shows God creating the sun and moon. At the time (1508–12), most Christians believed God created Heaven and Earth in six days.

THE WEEK

The week has nothing to do with the sun or moon. It was invented to mark the interval between market days, and so for many centuries a week could be of varying length in different cultures and parts of the world.

Our week has seven days, but many civilizations in the ancient world had weeks of a different length. Some African peoples had a four-day week. In Assyria, a week was five days long. In Egypt and among the Incas of Peru, it lasted 10 days. Around 700 B.C. the Babylonians chose the seven-day week, because seven was their lucky number. The Jews also had a seven-day week, because in the Bible, in the Book of Genesis, the story of the Creation tells how God made the world in six days and rested on the seventh.

THE MONTH

Since the first people looked at the night sky, they could see that the moon changed shape, from a new

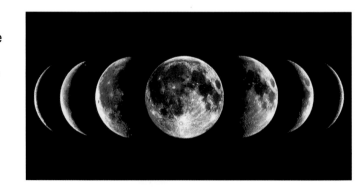

The phases of the moon from new to full and back again take just over 29 days. It gave people a useful time unit: the month.

OLYMPIC TIME

The Ancient Greeks counted in four-year cycles, known as the Olympiads. These corresponded to the Olympic Games, which were first held in 776 B.C. Each Olympiad was named after the supreme champion of the Games, and the three years leading up to each of the Games were simply numbered 1, 2, and 3.

moon to a thin crescent and then to a fat, round full moon. This is how the idea of a month came into being—a month is a "moon time."

The month can be measured in two ways. It can be the time taken for the moon to travel once around the Earth. It can also be the time the moon takes to pass through its complete cycle of changes—called "phases"—from new to full and back to new again. This phase month is called the synodic month and lasts 29.53 days. The moon takes 27.3 days to travel once around the Earth. This is called the sidereal month.

Our months have names that come from the old Roman calendar (see pages 11, 15, 17, and 19). Around the world, people gave the months different names. In Siberia, tribal peoples had a "Ducks and Geese Fly Away" month. Native Americans gave their months names such as "Deer Month."

▼ *Sandro Botticelli's 1480s painting of Venus and Mars was probably done to mark a spring wedding. Mars, the Roman god of war, gave his name to March. Venus (known to the Greeks as Aphrodite) was associated with April.*

THE NAMES OF THE MONTHS—2

▶**April** April gets its name from the Roman month Aprilis, so called either because the Romans thought the month sacred to the Greek goddess of love, Aphrodite, or from the Latin verb *aperire*, which means "to open"—as blossoms do in the spring

▶**May** May is another Roman month, named after the goddess Maia

▶**June** June comes from the Roman month Juniis, probably named after the goddess Juno *(see also pages 11, 17, and 19)*

The Romans' Problem

WHERE IS SPRING?

Our word "calendar" comes from a Roman word meaning "the first day of the month." Unlike the Egyptians, the Romans had no Nile flood to help them measure the farming year, so they had to create a calendar to help them.

The first Roman calendar had only 304 days, with a year of 10 months. The

true year was 365.25 days long. Since just over 61 days were missing, the Romans soon found that the calendar slipped behind the seasons. To catch up, the Romans added two extra months, increasing the year to 355 days. The new year began in Martius (March). But the year was still too short. March, a month that was supposed to be at the start of the farmers' sowing season, "wandered" until eventually it fell in early summer. The problem was getting worse year by year.

A Roman mosaic showing farmers in spring. The month should have been March, but by 50 B.C. March had moved into summer.

CAESAR'S RULES

The Romans tried adding a "bonus" month every other year. They called this extra month Mercedinus. But still their calendar didn't work. By the time Julius Caesar (c. 100–44 B.C.) was in charge, the Roman calendar was about three months out of step with the seasons. September fell in winter instead of in autumn.

In 46 B.C. Caesar sought the advice of an astronomer named Sosigenes to find out how to solve this problem, and as a result he ordered a new calendar to be made.

The new "Julian" calendar was made up of 12 months. The months had 30 and 31 days alternately (unlike the calendars used today), except for February, which had 29 days. Every fourth year, February was to have an extra day. This "leap year" of 366 days would make sure the calendar kept in step with the solar year. From then on, the new year would begin on January 1, not March 1 (see page 17).

Julius Caesar used his power as dictator of Rome to reform the calendar. No one argued with his changes, and most of Europe adopted the Julian calendar.

THE ROMAN MONTHS

The original months in the Roman calendar were Martius, Aprilis, Maius, Junius, Quintilis, Sextilis, September, October, November, and December. According to the Romans, this 10-month calendar was invented by Romulus, the legendary founder of Rome. King Numa Pombilius later added January and February. When January was made the first month of the year by Julius Caesar, the old seventh month (September) became the ninth, the eighth (October) became the tenth, and so on.

According to myth, Romulus and his brother Remus were raised by a she-wolf.

THE YEAR OF CONFUSION

To bring the calendar back in line with the seasons, Julius Caesar ordered the year 46 B.C. to last 445 days! Not surprisingly, Romans called this "the year of confusion." By the following year, however, 45 B.C. (remember, B.C. dates count backward), everything was normal again. The Julian calendar was used throughout Europe for the next 1,500 years.

NEW NAMES

The Romans renamed the fifth month—Quintilis, which had become the seventh month—calling it Julius (July), after Julius Caesar. In 8 B.C., Emperor Augustus decided he wanted his own month too, so the old sixth month—Sextilis—became Augustus (August). It was now the eighth month. Augustus did not want his month to be shorter than any others, so he took a day from February to give his month 31 days. February now had 28 days in a normal year and 29 in a leap year.

THE NAMES OF THE MONTHS—3

► **July** July is named after the Roman month Julius, named in honor of Julius Caesar

► **August** Another Roman emperor, Augustus, gave this month his name in 8 B.C.

► **September** September was the seventh month in the old Roman calendar; the name comes from *septem*, Latin for "seven" *(see also pages 11, 15, and 19)*

Movable Feasts

B.C. AND A.D.

The calendar used for everyday business in most parts of the world starts from an agreed date for the birth of Jesus Christ. Dates before the birth of Christ have the letters B.C. after them; this stands for "before Christ." The alternative form B.C.E., short for "before the common era," is used by some people.

So a person born 30 years *before* the "start date" has the birth year of 30 B.C. The year before this was 31 B.C.; the year after was 29 B.C.

Dates after the birth of Christ are preceded by A.D., short for the Latin *anno domini* ("in the year of our Lord"). Someone born 30 years *after* the birth of Christ has the birth year of A.D. 30. The year before was A.D. 29; the year after was A.D. 31.

There is no year zero. The year before A.D. 1 was 1 B.C.

The Wise Men with the baby Jesus, painted by Dutch artist Jan Mostaert in the early 1500s. For Christians, the birth of Jesus marked a new era, and the event became the marker from which all other events were recorded.

WHEN WAS JESUS BORN?

This dating system was begun by a monk named Dionysius Exiguus about A.D. 525. We do not know the precise day or even year of Jesus' birth. Scholars believe that Jesus was born between 4 and 1 B.C. (the year that King Herod the Great died). His birthday was first celebrated on December 25 sometime in the A.D. 300s.

MOVABLE FEASTS

In the Christian year, some special days occur on the same date every year. Christmas Day is always celebrated on December 25. Other special days are called "movable feasts" ("feasts" here means holidays or festivals) because the date on which they are celebrated changes every year. These movable feasts are based on the phases of the moon rather than on the solar calendar.

RINGING THE HOURS

Throughout the Middle Ages, the Church worked to a seven-hour day. It was based on the daily services of worship and prayer which were called matins, prime, terce, sext, none, vespers, and compline. The first bell-ringing clocks were made to warn monks when it was time for the next service to begin.

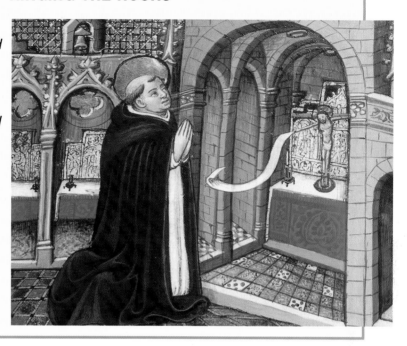

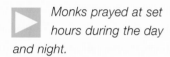 *Monks prayed at set hours during the day and night.*

EASTER

The oldest and most important Christian festival is Easter, which falls on a different date every year. The name "Easter" comes from an Anglo-Saxon spring goddess called Eostre, whose festival was celebrated in April.

In A.D. 325, a council of Christian leaders met at Niceae in Asia Minor (modern Turkey). This council decided that Easter should be celebrated on the first full moon on or after the spring equinox (the day on which there are equal hours of darkness and light). This means that Easter can fall any time between March 22 and April 25. The Eastern Orthodox Church, however, fixed its Easter as the first Sunday after the Jewish festival of Passover.

Lighting candles for Easter in Greece. Easter is the chief festival of the Christian year, yet unlike Christmas it has no fixed date.

THE NAMES OF THE MONTHS—4

▶ **October** October was the eighth month in the old Roman calendar, from the Latin *octo*, meaning "eight"

▶ **November** November was the ninth month in the old Roman calendar, from the Latin *novem*, meaning "nine"

▶ **December** December was the 10th month in the old Roman calendar, from the Latin *decem*, meaning "10" *(see also pages 11, 15, and 17)*

Calendars, Calendars…

THE JEWISH CALENDAR

The Jewish calendar is based on the sun and moon, the earliest of which is the Gezer calendar, probably written during the reign of King Solomon in the late 900s B.C. After 587 B.C. (when they were taken as captives into Babylon), the Jews had to use the Babylonian calendar. They still use the Babylonian month names, slightly changed—for example, Nissan, from the Babylonian Nisan.

The Jewish calendar begins with the Creation, 3,760 years before the start of the Christian era. So to find what year it is in the Jewish calendar, you add 3,761 years.

Muslim pilgrims in Mecca, during the month of Zulhijjah. Many Muslims use the Christian calendar for business, but the Islamic calendar in private.

THE ISLAMIC CALENDAR

The Islamic calendar is also based on the moon. The crescent moon is an Islamic symbol. For Muslims (followers of Islam), the calendar begins with Muhammad's journey from Mecca to Medina in A.D. 622.

The first day of the month, Muharram, was fixed as the beginning of the Islamic year, corresponding to July 16, A.D. 622. The year has 12 moon months, alternately 30 and 29 days long. The year has 354 days, and so the months do not keep in step with the passage of the seasons. This means that Ramadan, the month of fasting, falls 10 to 11 days earlier every year. A devout Muslim must see the new moon before he or she can begin the fast, but in practice many people follow the ruling of a Muslim religious law expert who declares when Ramadan is to begin.

CHINA

According to legend, the Chinese emperor Huangdi invented the calendar in 2637 B.C., so this is the year from which the Chinese date it. The Chinese calendar is divided into cycles of 60 years each. The year 2002 is the 19th year of the 78th cycle. Years have names, part of which is the name of one of 12 animals. The animals come in this order in the cycle: rat, ox, tiger, hare, dragon, snake, horse, sheep, monkey, rooster, dog, and pig. Chinese months begin at the new moon. New Year starts at the second new moon after the beginning of winter.

A Chinese temple stone shows the yin-yang life-force symbol; around it are the 12 year animals (horse at the bottom).

JAPAN

The Japanese use the same calendar as we do in the West, but they split their history into epochs, linked to the reigns of emperors. The present epoch, Hesei, began in 1989, with the accession of Emperor Akihito.

INDIA

People in India use several calendars. The Vikrama era dates from 57 B.C. The Saka era dates from A.D. 78 and is the national calendar of India, running in step with the Western calendar. Buddhists have a calendar that dates from 543 B.C., the date of the death of Buddha. Jains and Parsees have calendars of their own, too.

THE MAYAN CALENDARS

The Mayan people of Central America used three calendars. The everyday calendar had 365 days. There were 18 months, each with 20 days, with an extra five days added. The Maya also had a sacred religious calendar of 260 days. The two calendars came together to start on the same day every 52 years. This was a very important event. Every 52 years people feared the sun might fail to return and the world would end.

   The Maya also had a third calendar, a complicated cycle equal to 5,130 years. The cycle we are in now ends in the year 2012, if experts have read the Mayan sign-writing correctly.

16th-century copy of the Aztec calendar stone.

A FATEFUL YEAR

In 1519, the Aztecs thought a god had come to visit. In the Aztec calendar, this was a "One-Reed Year," in which it was predicted that the white-skinned, bearded god Quetzalcoatl, the Feathered Serpent, would return to Mexico. When white-skinned, bearded men did indeed arrive, the Aztecs welcomed them. But the newcomers were no gods; they were Spanish conquistadors, led by Hérnan Cortez. The Spaniards conquered the Aztecs and destroyed their empire and their calendar.

The Lost Days

SLIPPING BEHIND

The Julian calendar, introduced by Julius Caesar, was used in Europe for more than 1,500 years. But there was still a problem, which was getting worse every year. The Julian year was about 11 minutes and 14 seconds longer than the sun year. As the centuries passed, the calendar and the seasons began to shift yet again. The Roman Catholic Church, Europe's most powerful organization, was concerned, and Church leaders worked out that there was a 10-day error.

By the 1580s, the spring equinox, fixed by the Council of Nicaea as March 21, had slipped back to March 11 on the calendar. This made life difficult for farmers: if they sowed seeds too early, crops would not grow well.

THE POPE STEPS IN

The Church was worried that its festivals were falling behind "real" time, so on the advice of experts in calendars and astronomy, Pope Gregory XIII ordered a revolution. The year 1582 would lose 10 days. October 4 would be followed by October 15. Also, in the future, no century years (such as 1700) would be leap years unless they could be equally divided by 400 (such as 1600).

BRITAIN AND AMERICA GO SLOW . . .

The new Gregorian calendar of 1582 was adopted by all Roman Catholic countries. But Protestant countries, including Britain, were slow to accept it. Britain and its American colonies stuck with the old-style Julian calendar until 1752. By then, it was 11 days out of step.

Pope Gregory XIII (1502–85) relied on two scientists, Luigi Ghiraldi of Italy and Christopher Clavius of Germany, to alter the calendar and to correct the errors that had appeared in the 1,600 years since Julius Caesar's calendar.

RUSSIAN REVOLUTION

Russia also lagged behind in switching to the new calendar. In 1699, Czar Peter the Great decreed that future new years would start on January 1 in Russia, not on September 1 as they had previously. The old Russian calendar, which had been numbered from the creation of the world, was abandoned, so the next year was to be 1700 rather than 7208! However, Peter stuck to the old-style Julian calendar, so it was not until 1918 that Russia finally caught up with the rest of Europe.

PETRO PRIMO
CATHARINA SECUNDA
MDCCLXXXII

. . . AND CATCH UP

In 1752, the British government decided to catch up. That year, September 2 was followed not by September 3, but by September 14. People felt time was being "stolen" from them, and angry mobs marched through city streets shouting, "Give us back our 11 days!"

The American statesman Benjamin Franklin told readers of his *Poor Richard's Almanac* to enjoy the extra 11 days in bed, although he would not have expected them to take him literally!

◄ *U.S. statesman Benjamin Franklin (1706–90) was very relaxed about the new Gregorian calendar when it came to the American colonies in 1752. "Losing" 11 days did not worry him —after all, Europe had managed since 1582.*

KEY DATES

▶ **1345** First attempts at calendar reform by Pope Clement VI
▶ **1517** Pope Leo X tries, but fails, to reform the calendar
▶ **1582** Pope Gregory orders the new Gregorian calendar to be used in Catholic countries
▶ **1752** Britain and its American colonies change to the Gregorian calendar
▶ **1873** Japan adopts the Western-style calendar
▶ **1918** Russia makes the change
▶ **1924** The Greek Orthodox Church adopts the Gregorian calendar
▶ **1949** China switches to the Gregorian calendar

Happy New Year

THE MILLENNIUM DID NOT BUG US

The Christian Gregorian calendar is now used throughout the world. It makes sense for people everywhere to have the same calendar in front of them, especially when doing business. Other calendars remain in use, but almost everyone sticks to the same year-date.

The end of a century (100 years) seems to mark a turning point. It is convenient to talk of "the 19th century" when discussing history, for example. The Millennium, marking the year 2000, was celebrated around the world, but most historians believe that Jesus Christ was born about 4 B.C., so the celebrations were four years late. And although the fireworks exploded at midnight on December 31, 1999, calendar experts pointed out that the new millennium could not start until January 1, 2001, when the 2,000th year actually ended. Most people had planned to celebrate too early!

Fireworks are a New Year's Eve tradition around the world, and the new millennium meant an extra-special send-off to the old year. A new year means a fresh start, with some good resolutions!

HAPPY NEW YEAR

People in most countries celebrate the new year with parties, parades, and merrymaking. They see the old year out on New Year's Eve. Throughout history, people have started the new year with a ceremony, such as putting out an old fire and lighting a new one. Many people make New Year resolutions, as a sign of a fresh start.

New Year's Day has not always been celebrated on January 1. In most countries of medieval Europe, the new year began on March 25—which was Annunciation or Lady Day for Christians. In England, before 1066, the Anglo-Saxons had kept December 25 as New Year. There are no references to calendars or dates in the New Testament of the Bible. Nowhere in the Bible is there any reference to New Year's Day.

The Jewish New Year is the solemn festival of Rosh Hashanah, and falls during September or early October, depending on the cycle of the moon.

The Muslim New Year also falls on different dates from year to year, because it is linked to the moon.

The Chinese New Year, also moon-cycled, is celebrated with noisy firecrackers and dancers wearing colorful dragon costumes.

FRENCH REVOLUTIONARY RULES

In 1792, the French Revolutionaries threw out the Gregorian calendar and introduced a new one. The new year began in autumn. It had 12 30-day months, followed by five holidays in ordinary years and six holidays in leap years. There was no week, each month being split into three 10-day periods, with the 10th day as a day off for workers. The revolutionary calendar was used until 1806, when Napoleon ordered a return to the Gregorian calendar.

THE FRENCH REVOLUTIONARY YEAR (1793)

Vendrémaire (vintage)   *September 22*
Brumaire (mist)   *October 22*
Frimaire (frost)   *November 21*
Nivose (snow)   *December 21*
Pluviose (rain)   *January 20*
Ventose (wind)   *February 19*
Germinal (seed time)   *March 21*
Floréal (blossom)   *April 20*
Prairial (meadow)   *May 20*
Messidor (harvest)   *June 19*
Thermidor (heat)   *July 19*
Fructidor (fruit)   *August 18*

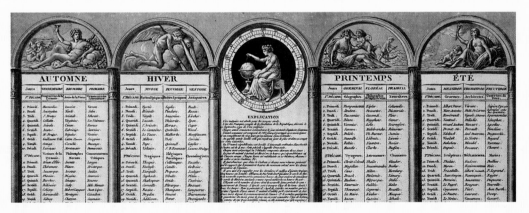

A French calendar of 1794, two years after the Revolutionary changes. It shows the four seasons, starting the year with autumn.

THE YEAR 2000 IN OTHER CALENDARS WAS . . .

- ▶ **Ancient Egyptian calendar**   year 6236
- ▶ **Jewish calendar**   year 5761
- ▶ **Buddhist calendar**   year 2544
- ▶ **Islamic calendar**   year 1420
- ▶ **Persian calendar**   year 1378

Diaries and Almanacs

BUSY, BUSY, BUSY

Every new year, many people buy or are given a diary. Most of us use our diaries to look up a date, remember a friend's birthday, or note an appointment. Busy people carry personal organizers, to help them keep track of vital addresses, phone numbers, and appointments.

KEEPING A PERSONAL DIARY

A personal diary is the writer's record of events and thoughts. It is not usually intended to be read by anyone else. A journal is similar, but is kept for people to read later: it might be an account of an ocean voyage or an exploring expedition, for example.

Old family diaries are interesting to historians, as well as to relatives. Some diaries give us revealing insights into the writer's life.

FAMOUS DIARIES

Probably the most famous English diarist is Samuel Pepys (1633–1703). He wrote about his work as a government official, but also about his home life and his escapades. From his diary, we learn what it was like to be in London during the Plague of 1665 and the Great Fire of 1666. To keep his diary private, Pepys wrote in a shorthand code, which was not broken until the early 1800s.

▼ *The Great Fire of London in 1666 was vividly described in the diary by Samuel Pepys. "It made me weep to see it," he wrote. "The churches, houses and all on fire and flaming at once . . . and a horrid noise the flames made."*

EXPLORERS' JOURNALS AND PERSONAL DIARIES

American explorers Meriwether Lewis and William Clark made an epic journey across the Rocky Mountains in 1804–6. Their journals contained maps, sketches, and descriptions of the Native Americans they met and the natural wonders they saw.

Personal diaries can be more light-hearted. Fanny Burney, an 18th-century English diarist, tells how she watched King George III sea-bathing while a band played "God Save the King."

Another English diarist was John Evelyn (1620–1796), who began his diary when he was 11 years old and kept it for over 70 years. In America, the diary of plantation-owner William Byrd the Second (1674–1744) describes life in the Virginia colony in the 18th century. Queen Victoria (1819–1901) kept a diary from childhood until she was a very old woman. Many politicians have kept diaries, which were later turned into books of memoirs.

Perhaps one of the most poignant diaries is that of Anne Frank (1929–45). Anne was a German-Jewish teenager, in hiding from the Nazis during World War II. Anne Frank's diary tells of her family's secret life in Amsterdam for two years, until they were betrayed and captured. Anne Frank died in a concentration camp. Her diary was published after the war.

Anne Frank's diary recorded her thoughts as she hid with her family from the Nazis. It was published in 1947, two years after her death.

ALMANACS

An almanac contains a calendar, dates of interest, and important events, as well as all kinds of facts. Some almanacs also give predictions about the future. Early almanacs provided a year calendar with eclipses, movements of the planets, and rising and setting times of the sun, moon, and stars. Such information was useful for farmers and sailors.

Benjamin Franklin published America's most famous almanac, *Poor Richard's Almanac*. It came out every year from 1733 to 1758, and in it Franklin gave witty and wise advice to his readers, such as "Early to bed, early to rise, makes a man healthy, wealthy, and wise."

What Day Is It?

SMALL WORLD

Air travel has made the world seem smaller. A journey that took several weeks by ship in the 1800s now lasts less than 24 hours by jet plane. We can travel so fast that our bodies need time to recover from "jet lag" and the confusion that having two or three breakfasts in one day can cause!

But we do not have to travel from home to explore distant places: we can make telephone calls, visit a web site, or watch live TV from the other side of the world. When we do this, we realize that time is not the same everywhere. When it's day in the United States, it's night in Australia.

Concorde speeds across the Atlantic Ocean in three hours. Allowing for a five-hour time difference, a passenger leaving London at 12 noon arrives in New York two hours before she set out!

TIME ZONES

Every hour, the sun appears to travel over 15 degrees (1/24) of the Earth's surface. This is because the planet is spinning like a giant top. Sun time changes as you move east or west. Every 15 degrees east of the Greenwich meridian a traveler must advance a watch by one hour. Going west, a traveler must set back a watch by one hour for every time zone crossed.

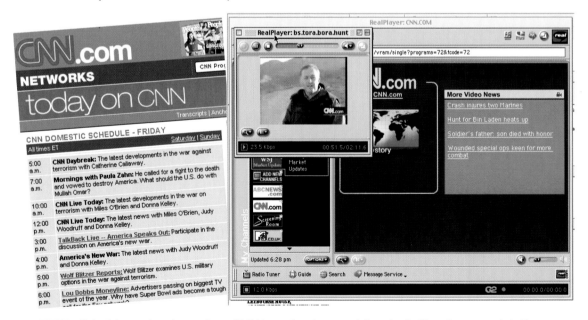

Television networks such as CNN broadcast around the clock. People can watch the news, send e-mails, or play computer games with friends in "real time" any hour of the day.

THE INTERNATIONAL DATE LINE

Halfway around the world from the Greenwich meridian is another imaginary line. This is the International Date Line. When you cross this imaginary line, you gain or lose a whole day. The date just to the west of the line is one day later than the date just to the east of the line.

The International Date Line runs across the Pacific Ocean. It follows the 180-degree meridian most of the way, but zigzags around country borders so that people in the same country do not have different calendar dates on the same day.

January

DO WE NEED A NEW CALENDAR?

We are still using the calendar Pope Gregory introduced in 1582. It gains nearly 26 seconds a year and is already nearly three hours ahead of true sun time. Sometime in the third millennium, this error will probably be fixed by getting rid of one leap year so that we will lose a day.

Some people think we should have a neater calendar, such as the so-called Universal or World calendar. This would have alternate months of 30 and 31 days. The new year would always start on a Sunday and each month would always start on the same day. Each leap year day would be a special World's Day. There have been other ideas, but it looks as if we will go on as we are for a few more years yet.

A FEW FAMOUS DATES

▶ **January 1** — New Year's Day
▶ **January 26** — Australia Day
▶ **February 14** — Valentine's Day
▶ **March 1** — St. David's Day (Wales)
▶ **March 17** — St. Patrick's Day (Ireland)
▶ **April 1** — April Fool's Day (this used to mark the end of New Year's celebrations)
▶ **April 23** — St. George's Day (England)
▶ **May 1** — May Day
▶ **July 1** — Canada Day
▶ **July 4** — Independence Day (USA)
▶ **July 14** — Bastille Day (France)
▶ **October 1** — China's National Day
▶ **October 31** — Halloween
▶ **November 5** — Guy Fawkes' Night (UK)
▶ **November 11** — Remembrance or Veterans' Day
▶ **November 30** — St. Andrew's Day (Scotland)
▶ **December 25** — Christmas Day
▶ **December 31** — New Year's Eve

Glossary

Astrologer
A person who believes the stars and planets shape our personalities and our future lives.

Astronomer
A scientist who studies the stars and planets through observation.

Aztecs
People who ruled an empire in Mexico until they were conquered by Spain in 1519.

Calendar
A chart or table showing the days, weeks, and months of the year.

Creation
A belief found in many religions that the world and living things were made by God.

Cycle
A series of events repeated in the same order.

Day
The time from sunrise to sunset; also the 24-hour day from midnight to midnight.

Degree
A unit of measurement (temperature or the angle of a circle, for example). A circle has 360 degrees.

Diary
A written record of daily thoughts and activities.

Dinosaur
A type of reptile now extinct.

Eastern Orthodox Church
A branch of the Christian Church, which split from Rome (the Western Church) in 1054.

Eclipse
The blocking of light from the sun or the moon. The moon may pass between the Earth and the sun (solar eclipse), or the Earth may block sunlight from reaching the moon (lunar eclipse). Eclipses were startling events in ancient times.

Festival
A special time of holiday or religious celebration.

Fossil
The remains of a long-dead animal or plant, preserved in rock.

French Revolution
Uprising in 1789 in which the people of France overthrew the monarchy and set up a form of republic.

Hindus
Followers of the Hindu religion, which has many gods and goddesses and is very ancient.

Jesus Christ
In Christianity, the Son of God; his teachings are the basis for the Christian faith.

Latin
The language of the ancient Romans, later used by the Church in Europe and by scholars.

Leap Year
Every four years, except those divisible by 100 but not 400; February has 29 days.

Maya
Ancient people of central America skilled in mathematics and astronomy.

Mesopotamia
The land between the rivers Tigris and Euphrates (modern Iraq), home of several important early civilizations.

Millennium
A period of 1,000 years, from the Latin *mille* (1,000) and *annus* (year).

Monk
A man who belongs to a religious order and lives in a monastery.

Month
A 12th part of a year, with 30 or 31 days. February has 28 days except in a leap year, when it has 29.

Muhammad
The prophet and founder of the religion of Islam.

Nile
The longest river in the world, flowing from central Africa northward through Egypt into the Mediterranean Sea.

Orbit
The path followed by a moon or planet as it moves around another body in space. The moon orbits the Earth, and the Earth orbits the sun.

Philosopher
A person who seeks wisdom and to understand the nature of life.

Planet
A large body in space orbiting a star.

Pope
The head of the Roman Catholic Church.

Roman Catholic Church
The largest and oldest of the Christian churches, with its headquarters in Rome.

Romans
Ancient people who ruled an empire that grew from Italy to control much of Europe, North Africa, and the Near East until its collapse in the A.D. 400s.

Seasons
Part of the year, such as the four seasons of cool countries—spring, summer, autumn, winter.

Shorthand
A quick form of writing, used for note-taking.

Solar
Meaning "of the sun."

Solstice
The moment each year when the sun is either at its most northerly (the shortest day) or most southerly position (the longest day); the winter solstice in the northern half of the world is around December 21; the summer solstice is around June 21.

Star
A huge ball of hot gas in space, giving off energy as light. The sun is a medium-sized star.

Sun
The star around which the nine planets of our solar system move in orbit.

Universe
Everything that exists in space, including all the stars and other matter in it.

Year
The time it takes for the Earth to make one orbit around the sun; our calendar year is made up of 365 days. Years on other planets are longer or shorter.

Index